Melbourne Australia Travel Guide

Attractions, Eating, Drinking, Shopping & Places To Stay

Brenda Armitage

Copyright © 2014, Astute Press
All Rights Reserved.

No part of this publication may be reproduced, stored in a retrieval system, or transmitted, in any form or by any means without the prior written permission of the publisher, nor be otherwise circulated in any form of binding or cover other than that in which it is published and without similar condition being imposed on the subsequent purchaser.

If there are any errors or omissions in copyright acknowledgements the publisher will be pleased to insert the appropriate acknowledgement in any subsequent printing of this publication.

Although we have taken all reasonable care in researching this book we make no warranty about the accuracy or completeness of its content and disclaim all liability arising from its use

Table of Contents

Melbourne 7
   Culture 8
   Climate & When to Visit 9
   Location & Orientation 9
      City Centre 10
      Southbank 10
      St. Kilda 11
      South Melbourne 11
      Carlton 12
      Fitzroy 12

Sightseeing Highlights 13
   Federation Square 13
   Australian Centre for the Moving Image (ACMI) 14
   Royal Botanic Gardens Melbourne 15
   National Gallery of Victoria 17
      NGV International 17
      The Ian Potter Centre 18
   Eureka Skydeck 88 18
   Melbourne Zoo 20
   Old Melbourne Gaol (Jail) 21
   Scienceworks 22
      The Lightning Room 22
      Melbourne Planetarium 22
      House Secrets 23
      Sportsworks 23
      Explore-a-saurus 23
      Transportation 23
      Opening Hours 24
   Beaches 24
      St. Kilda Beach 24
      Brighton Beach 25
      Port Melbourne, South Melbourne & Middle Park 25
      Kerford Road Beach 25
      Elwood & Williamstown Beaches 26
   Melbourne City Tourist Shuttle 26

Recommendations for the Budget Traveller 27
Places to Stay 27
Hotel Claremont Guest House 28
Greenhouse Backpackers 29
Habitat HQ 30
Melbourne Central YHA 31
Melbourne Metro YHA 32
Places to Eat & Drink 32
Andrew's Hamburgers 33
The Beach Albert Park 34
A Minor Place 35
39 Pizzeria & Degustation Bar 36
Bar Lourinha 37
Places to Shop 38
Smith Street, Collingwood 38
Bridge Road, Richmond 39
Queen Victoria Market 39
Melbourne Central 40
Bourke Street, CBD 41

Tasmania 43
Culture 44
Location & Orientation 46
Climate & When to Visit 49

Sightseeing Highlights 50
Hobart 50
Salamanca Place & Market 51
Royal Tasmanian Botanical Gardens 52
Tasmanian Museum & Art Gallery 52
Launceston 54
Cataract Gorge 54
Queen Victoria Museum & Art Gallery (QVMAG) 55
Historic Convict Sites 56
Port Arthur Site 57
Estates of Brickendon & Woolmers 57
Darlington Probation Station 58
Coal Mines Site 58
Cascades Female Factory 59
East Coach Beach Resorts 59
Bay of Fires 59
Bicheno 60

St. Helens 60
Swansea 61
Bruny Island **61**
Cradle Mountain - Lake St Clair National Park **63**
Hastings Caves **64**
The Nut at Stanley **65**

Recommendations for a Budget Traveller **66**
  Places to Stay **66**
   BIG4 Iluka 66
   Edgewater 67
   Hadley's Hotel 68
   Quality Hotel 68
   Edinburgh Gallery B&B 69
  Places to Eat **69**
   Cornelian Bay Boathouse 69
   Solo Pasta & Pizza 70
   Remi de Provence 70
   Stillwater River 71
   AAJ Indian Café & Restaurant 72
  Places to Shop **72**
   Island Markets 72
   Sidewalk Tribal 73
   Henry Jones Design Gallery 74
   Harvest Launceston Farmers' Market 74
   Design Centre Tasmania 75

Melbourne

Melbourne is Australia's second largest city and capital of the state of Victoria. The city has numerous galleries, parks, museums and theatres along with enjoyable beaches, cafes and shopping streets. Many people use the city as a base from which to explore the surrounding areas of the **Great Ocean Road** and the **Grampians National Park.**

About one million visitors come to the city every year. Walk through the several acres of parkland or take a break in the plentiful restaurants and bars. Visit the oldest building in Melbourne, the **Mitre Tavern**, which was built in the year 1837 or take a ride to the top of the tallest building, **Eureka Tower.**

Melbourne welcomes all with its city centre nature, its culture and its beauty. City heritage controls on the heights of buildings make Melbourne attractive-looking while highlighting its architecture. Melbourne has well-maintained gardens and features fine art and science museums. There is a free tourist bus service and some of the best sights are free. Melbourne is a nature lover's city. It offers paths for walking and bicycling at the beaches along with hotels which are often equipped with eco-friendly features.

Culture

Melbourne is one of the cultural centres of Australia and has Victorian architecture, theatres, parks, gardens, galleries and museums. The four million residents of the city are big fans of sports and cultural events. The city boasts an active live music scene and an impressive food and coffee culture. The people here tend to dress up more as the climate is more changeable and cooler than in Sydney.

Particularly important events in Melbourne include the **International Film Festival** which is held every August and the **Comedy Festival** which is held in April. The **International Art Festival** is held in October. There are many museums including those dedicated to immigration, science, banking, sports, film, railways and Chinese History.

Climate & When to Visit

The weather of Melbourne is often described as having "four seasons in a day" with lots of springtime and autumnal-type weather. The city receives about 24 inches of rainfall each year and the wettest month is usually October. An average summer day in Melbourne has a temperature of around 79-86° F (26-30° C). The inland suburbs tend to be hotter than the coastal areas which enjoy a refreshing southerly breeze. Daytime temperatures in summer can exceed 104 °F (40 °C) and heatwaves are quite common.

Location & Orientation

Melbourne is located in southeastern Australia and is surrounded by the Dandenong mountain range, the Yarra River and the Mornington Peninsula.

The population of the city is made up of people from all walks of life and Melbourne is a multi-cultural and affluent city with a several sub-communities. The city is home to people with their origins in countries like Italy and Greece (Melbourne has the largest Greek population outside of Greece) as well as other communities including Arabic, Muslim, Vietnamese, Latvian, Indian, Chinese, Portuguese, Spanish, Serbian and African.

City Centre

This is the business district of Melbourne and is the historical core built on the Yarra River. The area includes the newly developed region of Docklands towards the west. This district is the site of some big developments like the NGV arts precinct, shopping malls and buildings of historical importance. The most impressive feature in the city centre is Federation Square, which incorporates galleries, atriums, bars, cinemas, cafes, restaurants and business centres.

Southbank

This region is the hub of fine dining, the fabulous Crown Casino and is offers much to keep the tourist entertained.

It is located 1 km away from the central business district on the southbank of the Yarra River. The area features many striking high-rise buildings. The Victorian Arts Centre is one of the big attractions has somewhat resembles the Eiffel Tower of Paris. Other attractions include the Melbourne Convention Centre and the Aquarium. There is also a large number of restaurants, shops and cafes located here.

St. Kilda

St. Kilda offers great beaches and a vibrant nightlife. It is located to the south of the city centre and is close to Port Philip Bay. The largest tourist attractions include the beaches of St. Kilda and Elwood, St. Kilda pier, Botanical Gardens and Marina. The district also houses the historic amusement area of Lune Park and the beachfront area known as the Esplanade.

South Melbourne

South Melbourne consists of the old ports of the city as well as the town centre and the historically important Clarendon Street. South Melbourne is also home to the Royal Botanic Gardens and the Southgate leisure and shopping development. Also look for the famous Melbourne Cricket Ground (MCG) and the excellent restaurant district in and near Clarendon Street.

Carlton

This is the University district and is also famous for its cuisine. Lygon Street features a large number of shops, cafes and pizzerias and draws food and coffee lovers from all parts.

There is a wide range of stores visit. The Melbourne Zoo, the Royal Exhibition Building and the Melbourne Museum are also located in this district.

Fitzroy

Fitzroy, the smallest district of Melbourne, is unique due to its small lanes and narrow streets. One way streets are also common here, making driving more complicated. The entertainment centre of Fitzroy is Brunswick Street, which is a major eating, entertainment and shopping area in Melbourne. The nearby Gertrude and Smith Streets are also well known for their great cafes and vintage stores.

Sightseeing Highlights

Federation Square

Corner Swanston & Flinders St
Melbourne
Victoria 3000
+ 613 9655 1900
http://www.fedsquare.com/

Federation Square is one of the largest free attractions of Melbourne.

It comprises an entire block of the city and is the work of Australian architects Bates Smart in association with Lab Architecture. It offers a unique combination of cultural and civic activities and has been recognized all over the world as one of the great public spaces.

Federation Square plays host to more than 2000 events every year. The square is always buzzing with exhibitions, performances, events, festivals, concerts, forums and fashion shows. The square is most conveniently located opposite the Flinders Street Station in the city centre (also an iconic Melbourne sight).

Australian Centre for the Moving Image (ACMI)

Corner Swanston & Flinders St
Melbourne
Victoria 3000
+61 (03) 8663 2200
http://www.acmi.net.au/

Immerse yourself in the world of television, digital culture and film at the Australian Centre for the Moving Image. It is home to the popular film festivals of Melbourne and special programs for kids and seniors as well as showing classic movies. ACMI hosts a free exhibition known as **Screen Worlds** along with hosting international and Australian cinema.

Visit the largest screen gallery in the world to see the exhibition or watch films in any of the auditoriums or hear from leading film and TV personalities. A ticket for a movie costs around $15.

There is a bar/café overlooking the Federation Square and the ACMI store which offers interesting merchandise for movie buffs.

Catch a train to the Flinders Street Station to reach the ACMI. You can also catch a tram to Flinders Street Station. The ACMI is open everyday from 10 am to 6 pm. It is closed on 25th December.

Royal Botanic Gardens Melbourne

Birdwood Ave
South Yarra
Victoria 3141
+61 – 03 9252 2300
http://www.rbg.vic.gov.au/

The Royal Botanic Gardens of Melbourne is a free attraction of the city and attracts over 1.6 million visitors a year. The gardens are a place of delight and discovery and feature a stunning collection of plants and peaceful lakes.

The garden is home to plant collections like succulents, roses, camellias, herbs, cycads, Chinese Plants, Californian plants, rainforest flora, cacti and perennials. The **Guilfoyle's Volcano** is a newly launched precinct for visitors. The garden also acts as a sanctuary for wildlife including eels, black swans, cockatoos, kookaburras and bell birds.

The **Ian Potter Foundation Children's Garden** is a popular attraction for children. The garden has everything a child could ever want. It features crawling tunnels, a forest in which to play hide-and-seek and it rocks for climbing.

The garden hosts tours and walks for visitors wanting to learn about the cultural significance and the history of the garden. Tours start from the Observatory Gate meeting point. After enjoying the beauty of the garden take a break at the Observatory Café or the Terrace Tearooms.

You can take a tram (numbers 5, 8, 16 or 67) from Flinders Street Station and get off at Domain Junction to reach the Royal Botanic Gardens.

The Royal Botanic Gardens are open everyday from 7:30 am to 8:30 pm. The Ian Potter Foundation Children's Garden is open through Wednesdays to Sundays from 10 am to 4 pm. It is closed during the school holidays of July.

National Gallery of Victoria

180 St Kilda Rd
Melbourne
Victoria 3004
+03 8662 1555 (10am-5pm)
http://www.ngv.vic.gov.au/

The National Gallery of Victoria consists of two galleries located at a short distance from each other and both of them are free to enter. The NGV stretches from St Kilda Road to the Federation Square and consists of the NGV International, the Arts Centre and the Ian Potter Centre all located a short walk from one another.

NGV International

180 St. Kilda Road, Melbourne

NGV displays the best of Asian, European, American and Oceanic Art. Since the time the gallery was opened in the year 1968, the collection has almost doubled. The building is one of the most iconic in Melbourne and the gallery has been revamped to house one of the most significant collections of the world.

The Ian Potter Centre

NGV Australia at Federation Square

The Ian Potter Centre is home to art of Australian origin from the present to colonial times. There is more Australian art on display here than in any other gallery in the world. The Ian Potter Centre also features a restaurant and a café.

Take tram numbers 1, 5, 6, 22, 64 or 72 from St Kilda Road/Swanston Street and get off at the Victorian Arts Centre Stop. You can also take a train to Flinders Street Station and walk from there. The NGV International is open from Wednesday to Monday from 10 am to 5 pm and remains closed on Tuesdays.

Eureka Skydeck 88

7 Riverside Quay
Southbank, Victoria 3006
+03 9693 8888
http://www.eurekaskydeck.com.au/
$18.50 (Adult)
$14 (Concession)

There is nothing to prepare you for the sight from the top of highest building in Australia, the Eureka Tower. It is a must-visit for visitors to Melbourne. The two elevators take you to the top of the building in less than a minute and then you are propelled to the **Edge**, a sliding cube made of glass (with the visitors inside!)

In addition to the unparalleled view, the Eureka building will keep you entertained with other interesting activities. You can visit the wall displays, experience the 6 metre Table of Knowledge or simply enjoy taking breathtaking pictures from the terrace.

The Eureka Skydeck 88 is open throughout the year from 10 am to 10 pm and is 5 minutes from Flinders Street Station. Just cross the bridge over the river to get there.

Melbourne Zoo

Elliott Ave
Parkville, Victoria 3052
+1300 966 784
http://www.zoo.org.au/melbourne
$26.10 (Adults)
$20.20 (Concession)

Melbourne Zoo is home to more than 250 species of animals from all over the world. The beautiful landscape of the zoo adds to the large variety of the animals located there. Walk around the African and Asian rainforests settings of the zoo to see the monkeys swinging from the trees and the tigers roaming. Stop to watch the orangutans performing their antics or explore the kangaroos, koalas, wombats or platypus and the other unique animals in an Australian bush setting. One of the most recent additions to the zoo is the Wild Sea which displays the penguins of Victoria, the Fur Seals of Australia and other animals which are native to the land. There is also a special enclosure for baboons which opened in 2011 and acts as the home to Hamadryas Baboons.

Melbourne Zoo is located at the city centre near Royal Park and can be easily reached by taking Tram 55 or by taking a train to the Royal Park Station from Flinders Street Station.

The zoo is open from 9 am to 5 pm everyday.

Old Melbourne Gaol (Jail)

377 Russell St (between La Trobe St and Victoria St)
+61 3 8663 7228
http://www.oldmelbournegaol.com.au
$23 (Adult)
$18 (Concession)

The Old Melbourne Gaol is the jail that was used to hold some of Melbourne's criminals in the 19th century (including the famous Ned Kelly). When the jail was built in the 1800's, it used to dominate the skyline of Melbourne. Some of the most dangerous criminals were held inside the jail along with homeless people, petty offenders and the mentally ill. The jail witnessed as many as 133 executions between the years of 1842 and 1929, when it was closed down.

Today the old Melbourne Gaol can be visited to see how its inhabitants were treated back then. The tour of the jail is mostly self-guided and consists of a visit to the cells along with film shows. The bones and face mask of Ned Kelly are on display.

Take Tram 24 to stop number 7 or tram 30 to La Trobe Street. You can also take a train to Melbourne Central Station and walk a few minutes to reach the jail.

The Old Melbourne Gaol is open everyday from 9:30 am to 5 pm and is closed on Good Friday and Christmas day.

Scienceworks

2 Booker St
Spotswood, Victoria 3015
+1300 130 152 (9 am to 5 pm)
http://museumvictoria.com.au/scienceworks/
$10.00 (Adults)

With a wide range of scientific displays and exhibitions on offer, Scienceworks will keep you entertained for hours. You can be a part of the informative tours or experience the live demonstrations. Let us take a look at all that Scienceworks has to offer:

The Lightning Room

The Lightning room gives you a hands-on experience about how lightning is formed and what happens when it strikes the earth. Discover all of this by watching a live show (30 minutes) which is both entertaining and informative.

Melbourne Planetarium

The Melbourne Planetarium takes you closer to the stars as you recline in your seat to watch some of the most stunning live scenes from outer space.

House Secrets

Explore the scientific facts behind everything you have at your home, from your washing machine to the food that you put in your mouth at the House Secrets.

Sportsworks

Sportsworks features 20 sporting challenges to help you to discover your sporting talents and body profile.

Explore-a-saurus

Explore-a-saurus is one of the newest additions to Scienceworks and you can discover everything about dinosaurs here. Here you will see comparisons of the types of plants they ate to the recreation of the sound they used to make.

Transportation

Take a train from Williamstown and Werribee line and get down at the Spotswood station. Scienceworks is located at just a distance of 10 minutes from there.

Opening Hours

Scienceworks is open everyday from 10 am to 4:30 pm and is closed on Good Friday and Christmas Day.

Beaches

Many beaches in Melbourne are watched over by lifesavers during the summer months, public holidays and school holidays.

St. Kilda Beach

St. Kilda is one of the most popular beaches of Melbourne and is great for swimming and other water activities. The St. Kilda Pier is good for viewing the skyline of the city and also for watching the sunset in the evening. There is regular ferry service to Southbank and Williamstown and the marina also offers boating facilities. The area near to the beach has facilities for barbecues and picnic tables. There are also paths for walking, rollerblading and bicycling.

Brighton Beach

This long stretch of sandy beaches includes Middle Brighton, Dendy Street and Brighton beaches. The region is well known for the colorful huts at the beach-edge. There are also great facilities for playing and barbecuing. Other options include yachting, windsurfing and boating. There are also paths for cycling and walking.

Port Melbourne, South Melbourne & Middle Park

These three beaches are close to the central part of Melbourne and are beautifully wide and sandy. They include paths for bicycling and walking as well as playgrounds. The Middle Park Beach is very popular for activities like beach volleyball and kitesurfing.

Kerford Road Beach

Kerford Road is very popular beach and has zones to exclude power skiing, sail boarding and boating so offer more protection for swimmers. There are also paths for cycling and walking along with a playground.

Elwood & Williamstown Beaches

These beaches are great for sailing, boating and swimming. There are also boat ramps and cycling and walking paths located nearby along with reserves for play, picnic and barbecue.

Melbourne City Tourist Shuttle

Corner of Flinders & Swanston streets
Melbourne, Victoria 3000
+03 9658 9658
www.thatsmelbourne.com.au/gettingaroundthecity/visitorassistance/pages/touristshuttle.aspx

The Melbourne City Tourist Shuttle is a service that is free for visitors to the city.

The bus stops at thirteen tourist attractions in the city and you have the option of getting on or off at any of the stops. The 13 stops include Federation Square, Chinatown Precinct, University of Melbourne, Arts Precinct, Lygon Street Precinct, Sports Precinct, Melbourne Museum, Queen Victoria Market, Southbank and Yarra River, Etihad Stadium, Victoria Harbor, Docklands, Waterfront City, Docklands, William Street, The Shrine and the Royal Botanic Gardens.

The free bus service runs daily from 9:30 am 4:30 pm every 30 minutes. There is no service on Good Friday and Christmas Day.

Recommendations for the Budget Traveller

Places to Stay

Melbourne provides accommodation options for every type of budget. It doesn't matter whether you are looking for a backpackers hostel or a luxury hotel; there is no dearth of accommodation in the city. Let us take a look at some recommended places to stay.

Hotel Claremont Guest House

189 Toorak Rd
South Yarra
Victoria 3141
+03 9826 8000
www.hotelclaremont.com
$60 - $ 149 per night

Hotel Claremont Guest House is unique in offering budget accommodation whilst being located in a multi-million dollar property It is a 77-room Victorian style guest house especially catering to budget travelers. Spend less on your resting place and more on sightseeing and shopping by staying here!

The guest house offers a 24 hour reception, 77 large, bright rooms, free WIFI, book exchange, internet café, telephone, a pharmacy on the premises, television in all the rooms, guest lounge and complimentary coffee and tea. All towels and bed linen are provided by the hotel and the rooms are serviced once a week. Breakfast is included in your room rate and consists of toast, fruit, cereals, coffee, tea and fruit juice.

Greenhouse Backpackers

Level 6, 228 Flinders Lane
Melbourne, Victoria 3000
+03 9639 6400
Toll Free: 1800 249 207
www.greenhousebackpacker.com.au
$32 - $35 per night (Dorms)
$80 - $90 per night (Private Rooms)

The Greenhouse Backpackers is located in Flinders Lane and is close to the entertainment district and shopping spots of Melbourne. The hostel boasts of a helpful and friendly staff along with clean and discounted dorms and private rooms to all the guests. Other facilities offered by the hostel include a Mega-Melbourne Walking Tour on Mondays, free WIFI, daily breakfast of cereals, toast, milk, tea or coffee. They offer free pancakes on Sundays at 11 am, a free dinner on Tuesday nights (Australian Barbecue or Pasta) and a big English breakfast on Thursdays.

Habitat HQ

333 St Kilda Rd
St Kilda, Melbourne
Victoria 3182
+ 03 9537 3777
Toll Free - 1800 202 500
www.habitathq.com.au
$28-$144 per night

Habitat HQ has been recognized as the best budget accommodation in Victoria. It is located in St Kilda and provides more than just a comfortable sleeping experience. The hostel is close to cafes, restaurants and bars as well as to the beaches of St Kilda. The hostel offers various other facilities like free daily music events, free WIFI, free breakfast, free keyboard and music guitars for use and free pick-up from the airport!

The hostel also offers free parking and is well known for its love of music. You can rent DVD's and watch them in the comfort of your room and don't miss the terrace view of the sunset. There is a huge guest lounge where you can hang out beside a cozy fireplace. The facilities offered are great and rooms are clean. There is an herb garden and an outdoor courtyard to relax in.

Melbourne Central YHA

562 Flinders Street
Melbourne, Victoria 3000
+613 9621 2523
http://www3.yha.com.au/Hostels/VIC/Melbourne-Hostels/Melbourne-Central-Hostel/
$30-$105 per night

This is where you should stay to be close to many of the tourist attractions in Melbourne.

The Melbourne Central YHA Hostel is located in Flinders Street and is very close to the Yarra River and Federation Square. It makes for a quiet bustling stay and provides a good alternative to the rather quiet stays offered by some of the other hotels nearby. The facilities include lounges on all floors, kitchens, high speed internet access and flat screen televisions. There is also a large rooftop deck and daily food and drink specialties. Some other facilities include a bar, a café, a food store and a 24 hour reception.

Melbourne Metro YHA

78 Howard Street
North Melbourne, Victoria 3051
+ 61 3 9329 8599
http://www3.yha.com.au/Hostels/VIC/Melbourne-Hostels/Melbourne-Metro-Hostel/
$30-$105 per night

Melbourne Metro YHA is located in North Melbourne and offers a panoramic view of the city from its rooftop BBQ and lounge. The hostel features electronic thermostats, solar hot water and an extensive recycling program. It has been accredited by the eco-tourism board of Australia.

The hostel also includes an ATM, Skype, WIFI, bicycle hire and a café. You can enjoy free events and activities, free DVD rental, electronic door locks and 24 hour access to the hotel. Some other facilities include a reading room, barbeque, video, television and parking.

Places to Eat & Drink

Melbourne is a multi-cultural city and this is reflected in the plethora of cafes, restaurants and bars in the city. The eclectic dining scene has something from every corner of the world. There are some popular dishes which are found everywhere as well as others which you may have never eaten before. Here are a few good choices:

Andrew's Hamburgers

144 Bridport St
Albert Park, Victoria 03206
http://www.andrewshamburgers.com.au/
Less than $15 per meal

Andrew's Hamburgers is a small café where there are usually five cooks working in a kitchen that is no bigger than the hallway of a house. Spend some time watching them work as they (usually) manage to do everything smoothly and without bumping into each other!

The most popular burger on their menu is "beef burger with the lot" which means ground beef, tomato, bacon, egg, a bun and mayonnaise served with tomato sauce for $9.50.

Andrew's Hamburgers remains crowded pretty much all the time so prepare to wait half an hour for your food. Lunchtime is from 11:30 am to 2:30 pm and dinner is from 5 pm to 9 pm.

The Beach Albert Park

97 Beaconsfield Parade
Albert Park, Victoria 3206
+61 3 9690 4642
http://thebeachalbertpark.com.au/
$16.00 - $25 (main course) $7.50 (desserts)

As the name suggests, The Beach Albert Park offers some great food along with a magnificent view of the beach. You can sit with a drink and quietly watch the waves hitting the shore. The restaurant offers both indoor and outdoor dining we'd recommend the latter.

The beach changes from a laid back eatery to a busy night spot. There is enough space for everybody and you will often find groups chatting the night away. The designer chairs and couches are something to see. The bar opens onto the beach with a beautiful courtyard. A meal for two with a glass of wine will come to about $29 each. The restaurant also offers pizzas and specialty meals for kids. The Beach Albert Park remains open daily from 10 am until late.

A Minor Place

103 Albion Street
Brunswick, Victoria 3056
+61 3 9384 3131
http://www.aminorplace.com.au/
$6.50-$14

A Minor Place has a large following because of its all day breakfast and Atomica coffee. It is tucked away in a corner in Brunswick, a suburb of Melbourne.

It is everything that a corner café should be. The hot favorites of A Minor Place include toasties, wraps and pides (Turkish bread). The signature dish is Henry's White Beans which is served with toast and dukkah (Egyptian spice mix). The bread served here is organic and the coffee is a special Atomica Blend. The desserts include delicacies like Lemon Tart, Vanilla Cupcakes, Vegan Muffins and Carrot cake. The Minor Place is open through Mondays to Saturdays from 8 am to 5 pm and on Sundays from 8:30 am to 4 pm.

39 Pizzeria & Degustation Bar

362 Little Bourke Street
Melbourne, Victoria 3000
+61 3 9642 0440
http://www.plus39.com.au/
$10 - $22 (Lunch) $10 - $22 (Dinner)

39 is a bar, pizzeria and restaurant with a distinct focus on Italian flavors. It is a simple place that combines the modern and the rustic and can accommodate only a small number of people at any one time. It is a great place for both lunch and breakfast and it offers tasty piadinas (Italian flatbread) with combinations like goats cheese and a selected variety of pizzas at just $10. Other popular options include the lobster and caviar pizza and the fresh Italian salumi (Italian cured meat) and cheeses. The latter can be used for complementing your pizza or as a meal in itself. Lunchtime dishes start at $12 and main courses for dinner time starts at $18. 39 Pizzeria and Degustation Bar is open everyday from 7 am to 10:30 pm.

Bar Lourinha

37 Little Collins St
Melbourne, Victoria 3000
(03) 96637890
http://www.barlourinha.com.au/
$24-$35 (Entrée and Main)

Bar Lourinha is an stylish bar which almost looks like a temple. The bar menu features a long list of exotic wines which make perfectly compliment the small plates which come for as little as $12. The bar offers cocktails like Montenegro, Punch di Fiamma, Mint and Lemon and Watermelon. There are also Spanish, Japanese and Italian wines available at the bar.

The tapas (small plates) served at the bar are changed according to the day of the week and the season. Some of the best dishes being Paella (Spanish rice) on Wednesday and Lamb on Mondays. Remember to book ahead because the bar is crowded at most times of the day. It is closed on Sunday's.

Places to Shop

Melbourne has huge shopping malls like the Melbourne Central as well as many small shops hidden away in quaint alleyways. If there is anything you ever wanted to buy, chances are that you will find it in Melbourne. A must visit for any shopaholic is the shopping triangle of the city between the Melbourne Central, the Queen Victoria Market and the Melbourne GPO. Following are some of the best shopping spots in Melbourne:

Smith Street, Collingwood

Smith Street
Fitzroy, Melbourne, Victoria 306
http://www.smithstreet.org.au/

Smith Street is the place to go for buying leisure, outdoor and sports gear. It is easy to get good deals on branded shoes, outdoor clothes and gym wear. Other than all of these, there are various shops where you can get good deals on fashionable clothes. There are some factory outlets between Alexandra Parade and Johnston Street.

You will find everything from accessories to jewelry here. You can reach Smith Street by catching tram number 86 from the city. It runs from 5am in the morning till midnight.

Bridge Road, Richmond

Melbourne, Victoria 3121
http://www.bridgerd.com.au/

Bridge Road is an established discount shopping area in Melbourne and is immensely popular with both locals and tourists. Along with several stores selling clothes, accessories and shoes at sale prices, the shopping area also offers great bars and cafés. Bridge Road is home to fashion boutiques which offer personal customer service and quality pieces at attractive prices. There is also a wide range of stores offering home furnishings featuring both antiques traders and furniture designers. You can reach Bridge Road by taking tram numbers 48 or 75 from the city centre. There are also tram numbers 79 and 78 from St Kilda and South Yarra respectively.

Queen Victoria Market

513 Elizabeth St
Melbourne, Victoria 3000
03 9320 5822
http://www.qvm.com.au/

The Queen Victoria Market is the mecca of shopping in Melbourne. It represents much more than just a market to the residents of the city. It is an institution, a historical landmark and a great tourist attraction all rolled into one.

The market has twice made its way to the final list for the Victorian Tourism Awards (2010 and 2011). Whether you buy baggage or clothing, you will get great items at low prices. The market is segmented into sections including the Deli Hall, Fruit and Vegetables, General Merchandise, Elizabeth Street Shops, Vic Market Place Food Court, The Meat Hall, Victoria Street Shops, The Wine Market and Organics.

You can reach the Queen Victoria market by catching any tram which goes to William Street. It remains closed on Mondays and Wednesdays.

Melbourne Central

211 Latrobe St
Melbourne, Victoria 3000
03 9922 1123
http://www.melbournecentral.com.au/

Melbourne Central is a modern shopping centre spread across several levels. The shopping centre boasts major brands as well as food and entertainment centres.

It is also famous for a giant pocket watch which makes all aware of its presence every hour. The shopping centre offers a wide range of choices in terms of food, culture, entertainment and fashion. There are several stores showcasing both international and Australian designers. The centre boasts more than 300 stores and has something to offer to both window shoppers and shopaholics alike.

Getting to the shopping centre is quite easy because it is located in the central business district of Melbourne You can catch the free tram service or any tram from St Kilda Road to Swanston Street to stop number eight.

Melbourne Central remains open from Monday to Saturday from 10 am to 6 pm with the exception of Friday when it is open till 9 pm. It remains open from 10 am to 3 pm on Sundays.

Bourke Street, CBD

231 Victoria Road, Fairfield
Melbourne, Victoria 3078
Australia
+61 3 9489 8884
http://www.bourkestreet.com.au/

Bourke Street is the entertainment hub of Melbourne and is viewed as the second most important street in the city. It is great for both budget shoppers and also for visitors with money to splurge. The street is bustling with activity and boasts a huge range of stores, cafes and restaurants. Take a walk down some of the nearby streets and you will find good deals in the small and independent stores. The GPO building located nearby has some tasty treats awaiting you after you are finished shopping.

The street is open only to shoppers and trams so always listen out for the tram bells before walking from one store to another. You will find everything from beauty products to fashionable handbags all at the same place. There is also the **Bourke Street Mall** located nearby for some more shopping.

You can take tram 86, 95 or 96 to reach Bourke Street and it remains open everyday from 10 am to 10 pm.

Tasmania

Tasmania is the smallest and only island state in Australia. Nearly half of Tasmania's archipelago of 334 islands are protected. The national parks and UNESCO World Heritage sites make Tasmania a popular destination for tourists.

Tasmania lies to the south of the state of Victoria across the Bass Strait and was discovered in the mid 17th century by the Dutch explorer, Abel Tasman. Although Abel initially named the island after his sponsor – Anthony van Diemen; the island was officially renamed by the British to Tasmania in 1856. Wild at heart and beauty, Tasmania is promoted to the visitors as 'A World Apart, Not A World Away'. This natural state is also known as 'The Island of Inspiration'.

Tasmania, with large areas of dolerite (surges of magma in volcanic zones), has a stunningly beautiful landscape with lots of colourful wildlife. The island is divided into a number of regions. The most populous region is Southern Tasmania with the capital and 2nd oldest Australian city – Hobart. The region also includes the picturesque Port Arthur. Northern Tasmania is more mountainous and is home to the popular Tamar Valley. The North West Coast region has a few coastal towns but is more popular for the scenic inland areas. The South West Coast region is a nature lover's delight with the whole area protected as a national park. Whereas the East Coast region is visited for the stunning beaches, the West Coast has the historic mining centers. Tasmania also has two extremely scenic islands in its Bass Strait Islands region.

Tasmania has something to offer for everyone. From basking in the sun in one of its stunning beaches and taking a guided nocturnal penguin-watching tour, to walking through the heritage national parks and enjoying the locally made wines and ciders, Tasmania is truly a world apart.

Culture

Tasmania is inhabited by about half a million people and there are more than a dozen annual events that keep the cultural calendar full. The summer month of January has the Cygnet Folk Festival. During this festival in Port Cygnet in the 2nd weekend of January, various performances and exhibitions on art, dance, and music are held in different venues across town.

The MONA Festival of Art and Music in January is a celebration of art and sound through theatre, dance, and visual art. The winter version of this festival – held in June – is called the Dark MOFO. February and March has the Australian Wooden Boat festival in Hobart, and the MS Fest music festival in Launceston.

The winter months have a number of festivals and events including the 6-day Targa Tasmania Road Rally. The popular agricultural festival of Agfest - http://www.agfest.com.au/ - is a celebration of the farming and produce of the land. Originally held in the mainland, the fest is now an important part of the Tasmanian calendar. A major multi-art form festival – Ten Days on the Island - http://www.tendays.org.au/ is held all over the state with a 100 venues and over 250 individual events. Music lovers can enjoy the Antarctic Midwinter festival and the Davenport Jazz festival in June and July. Similar to the Agfest, the Royal Launceston Show and the Royal Hobart Show celebrate the rural exploits of Tasmania. Fun events like livestock judging and wood chopping along with plenty of food and games stalls keep the whole family amused. Food lovers can also attend the Taste of Tasmania - http://www.thetasteoftasmania.com.au/ at the Salamanca Market and the waterfront area during Christmas. This weeklong festival is the largest food and wine festival on the island and is attended by nearly half a million visitors – the same as the population of the island!

Classical music lovers can attend a performance of the Tasmanian Symphony Orchestra at the Federation Concert hall. The island also has a number of small bands and individual artists who perform classical music at various venues across town. At the other extreme, one can attend jigs by metal-bands like the renowned Tasmanian Psycroptic or Striborg.

Not handicapped by its geographic size, Tasmania has a strong literary culture. In the early days, the island is found as a subject of writings of many discoverers and explorers. The landscape and the lives of the Aboriginal people provided inspiration to those writers. Over the years, Tasmania became home to many authors and there is a growing interest in literature on the island. The government promotes literature through many art festivals and book launches throughout the year.

Sport is a popular pastime of the island state and there are a variety of sporting events to choose from. Hobart is a popular international venue for cricket and features many important matches of the state and national team. The Aurora Stadium is home to the Australian Rules Football, a very popular sport in this part of the world. The 5-day Sydney to Hobart Yacht Race that starts on Boxing Day is not just a local event but a major tourist attraction. Soccer and tennis are 2 other popular sports that is closely followed and played in Tasmania.

Location & Orientation

The island of Tasmania is located to the south of the Australian mainland, off the coast of the state of Victoria.

The closest major mainland city is Melbourne. Separated by the Bass Strait, it is connected regularly by ferry services from the mainland.

Tasmania is served by 2 airports – the Hobart International Airport (IATA: HBA) - http://www.hobartairport.com.au/ and the Launceston Airport (IATA: LST) - http://www.launcestonairport.com.au/. These are 2 of the fastest growing airports in the country and although they do not have a regular schedule of international flights they have all the facilities and amenities of international terminals. These airports are also very important for their location; connecting the country with the continent of Antarctica. A recent growth in the services of low-cost airlines has seen a sharp rise in the passenger count in both these airports. Hobart airport has shuttle buses that operate to and from the city for every flight. It is run by Redline - http://www.tasredline.com.au/. Taxis and rental cars are also available. Launceston Airport also has a shuttle service (Tel: 03 6343 66 77) connecting the airport to the town in a 15-minute commute costing $18 (Australian dollar). The usual taxi and rental car service is also available.

A popular and common way to reach Tasmania from the mainland is through the ferry. The Spirit of Tasmania - http://www.spiritoftasmania.com.au/ runs regular ferry services connecting Melbourne and Devonport – the 3rd largest city in Tasmania.

Ferries usually start the journey around 8:00 pm and reach port next day at 7:00 am, both ways. Services are increased during peak seasons. These fully equipped ferries can even carry private vehicles. An adult ticket for the one way trip costs between $120 and $180. A car can be transferred for as low as $65 and bicycles for $7.

Once on the island, the best way to move around is with a private vehicle as the tourist pockets are spread all over the island. There are a number of car rental companies to choose from – Hertz - https://www.hertz.com.au/rentacar/reservation/, Avis - http://www.avis.com.au, and Sixt - https://www.redspot.com.au/. For those planning to drive, it has to be kept in mind that Australia has a left-lane driving rule. Speed limits are 110 km per hr for highways and 50 km per hr for built-up areas. Speed limits are strictly enforced and driving even 5 km above the speed limit will incur a fine. To drive in Australia, one must be 21 years of age and have an International Driver's License in English. While driving in Tasmania, especially through the inland highways, it is difficult to drive at the maximum speed limit because of the curves, strong winds, and poor road conditions. It is advisable to always keep some buffer when calculating the driving time. Cars can be brought from the mainland on the ferry.

For those opting for public transport can use the bus service run by Redline Tasmania - http://www.tasredline.com.au/, and Tassielink - http://www.tassielink.com.au/. Intra-city bus service is run by Metro Tasmania - http://www.metrotas.com.au/, and Merseylink - http://www.merseylink.com.au/.

However, it is to be kept in mind that bus services are not very frequent and could often be a long wait; the journey could also be tedious, for the distance and road conditions.

Climate & When to Visit

Tasmania experiences a cool temperate climate with summer between December and February when the average high is around 21 degrees Celsius and the average low around 12 degrees. Autumn months of March, April, and May see the climate getting cooler and wetter as winter settles in. Winter between June and August is cold and wet. The average high is around 12 degrees and low around 5 degrees. However, being a mountainous region, certain inland areas of high altitude can get colder and receive snowfall. Spring – between September and November – sees a transition from the cold and wet weather to considerably drier and warmer climate. The spring and summer months draw the maximum number of tourists to the island because of the warm and dry weather.

Sightseeing Highlights

Hobart

Located at the foot of the stunningly majestic Mt Wellington, Hobart is the smallest capital city of Australia and one of the most historic. Located in the south west of the island, Hobart is the 2nd oldest (after Sydney) and the coldest capital city of the island nation. In 2013, it was listed by Lonely Planet as one of the Top 10 Best in Travel cities in the world. With a great mix of history, culture, and art, Hobart is one of the most popular tourist destinations in Tasmania.

For those flying into the Hobart International Airport can take the shuttle to reach the city centre. The one-way trip costs $15. It is recommended to book tickets online at http://www.tasredline.com.au/ to avoid any delays at the airport. Taxis (approximately $45) and rental cars are also available. There is no public bus service from the airport with the closest bus route at a distance of about 5 km from the airport. Within the city, one can use the public bus service. The day ticket ($4.80) is recommended. The bus travels to most of the tourist attractions which can then be covered by foot. As the city limits are not too far, cycling is also a popular option.

Founded in 1804 as a penal colony along the banks of the River Derwent, Hobart today has many tourist attractions to choose from. A walk along the old streets will take past many beautiful Victorian and Georgian architecture. A short trip out of town takes one to many of the wineries of Hobart – there are even wine tours to choose from.

Salamanca Place & Market

Located in Sullivans Cove, Salamanca Place is a precinct in Hobart that is popular for the Saturday Market, and dozens of restaurants, galleries, pubs, and craft shops. The place is lined with rows of mid 19th century Georgian sandstone warehouses that now house many of the shops and eateries. Named after the Spanish town of the same name, Salamanca is the most vibrant part of Hobart and a must-visit if one is in town.

Every Saturday, the Salamanca Market (8:30 am to 3:00 pm) takes over the square. A visit to the market is a priority if one is in Hobart over the weekend. From clothes to accessories, and from local produce to unique handmade crafts, the Salamanca Market has it all. A perfect place to sit and watch people or have a relaxing glass of local wine after a bout of shopping, Salamanca scores high for all tourists visiting the island capital.

Royal Tasmanian Botanical Gardens

Located on a site that was once used by the Aboriginal people, the Botanical Gardens is an important conservation centre for plants and trees in Hobart. It was founded in 1818 and is home to a large collection of historic plants and trees, some well over a century old. The Gardens has the only Subantarctic Plant House in the world. The plants for this House have been collected from the heritage-listed Macquarie Island near Antarctica. Other than many exhibition sites, the Gardens also have a restaurant and a souvenir shop. Located near the Queens Domain, about 2 km from the Hobart CBD, the Wi-Fi enabled Botanical Gardens is open 7 days a week throughout the year. Entry to the Gardens is free; donation boxes are placed at various places in the Gardens for those who want to contribute.

Tasmanian Museum & Art Gallery

Established in 1843, the Tasmanian Museum & Art Gallery - http://www.tmag.tas.gov.au is the oldest 'Royal Society' outside England.

With some unique collections in geology, photography, historic coins, and decorative art, the museum attracts over 300000 visitors every year. Over the years the TMAG has established itself as a combination of museum, gallery, and herbarium; the largest of its kind in the country. There are a number of interesting and eye-catching permanent and floating exhibitions throughout the year. Located at Dunn Place, the TMAG is open from 10:00 am to 5:00 pm every day except Anzac day, Christmas Day, and Good Friday.

Other popular museums in Hobart include the Maritime Museum of Tasmania and the Museum of Old and New Art.

The city of Hobart has a number of other attractions in and around town. A hike or a drive to Mt Wellington enables guests to have a bird's eye-view of the city and its surroundings. Details of the weather conditions and access routes can be found at - http://www.wellingtonpark.org.au/. The Peppermint Bay -http://www.peppermintbay.com.au/, Cascade Brewery -http://www.cascadebreweryco.com.au/, Shot Tower, Cadbury's Chocolate Factory, and a number of winery tours are popular crowd pullers in town.

Hobart is also a place of culinary delight with its great wineries and fresh seafood and produce. Even if one cannot visit the wineries in the Coal River Valley or Huon Valley region, the city itself has many great places to savor the best in food and drinks.

Launceston

The city of Launceston is the 2nd largest city in the island of Tasmania. Founded in 1805, it is one of the oldest cities in the country, and like many other Australian cities, it is named after a British town, Launceston in Cornwall. Launceston (Australia) has many historic sites and buildings along with natural wonders in and around town that attract many visitors throughout the year. Just like the island capital Hobart, Launceston is also growing in to a major tourist centre in Tasmania. The small city attracts over half a million visitors annually with nearly a quarter of them coming from the UK.

Launceston has its own small airport - http://www.launcestonairport.com.au/ that has daily connections with Melbourne and Sydney. It is connected with Hobart and Devonport Port City through Highway 1. Once in Launceston, it is best use a rental car as public bus service is few and infrequent. Cycling is also a great option to move around town. However, most of the city attractions are within walking distance.

Cataract Gorge

Barely a 15-minute walk from the city centre along the River Tamar, this river gorge is a unique natural phenomenon in an urban setting. Once in the gorge, one can follow the pathway that was built in the late 19th century. This pathway – the King's Bridge-Cataract Walk - along the face of the cliff looks down onto the picturesque South Esk River.

The south side of the basin – called the First Basin - has an open area and a swimming pool. The area is surrounded by a bushland adjacent to the Launceston Beach. The contrasting north side – called the Cliff Grounds – is shadier and has a Victorian Garden with exotic plants and ferns. The 1972-chairlift across the river is the longest single-span chairlift in the world.

The Gorge is an ideal place for the whole family. This wild urban reserve has many interesting walks and trails that are perfect for a hike on a sunny day. A kiosk, restaurant, and rolling lawns provide ample opportunities for relaxation. One can also see peacocks and wallabies in the park area. Another interesting feature is the Duck Reach Power Station upstream. Commissioned in 1893, it was lighting Launceston by 1895 making it the first Australian city to be lit by hydro-electricity.

Queen Victoria Museum & Art Gallery (QVMAG)

The QVMAG http://www.qvmag.tas.gov.au was founded in 1891 and stands today as the largest museum outside a capital city in Australia. Located at 2 different sites – Royal Park and old Launceston Railway Workshops - within the city of Launceston, the museum has an excellent collection on colonial and contemporary Tasmanian art, natural sciences, history, and zoology. The QVMAG is basically divided into 3 sections, the museum, an art gallery, and a planetarium.

Exhibitions in the museum section include preserved railway workshops, the Sydney Cove shipwreck, and models of dinosaurs and death masks. The art gallery section has a number of exhibitions, some accompanied with guided tours. The planetarium was established in 1968 and now has enhanced viewing facilities with digital features after its renovation. The QVMAG also hosts many interactive events for children and adults throughout the year. The premise has a museum shop and a café. The QVMAG is open from 10:00 am to 4:00 pm every day (except Christmas Day and Good Friday). It has free entry.

Launceston offers a number of other attractions to its visitors. The City Park and historic streets are ideal for a relaxing stroll. The cruise or visits to the wineries of the Tamar Valley region are popular getaways for the locals and visitors alike. Launceston is a base to explore north Tasmania. Popular destination from the city includes the Tamar Island Wetlands, historic George Town, the coastal town of St Helens, the lavender farm of Scottsdale, and the Ben Lomond National Park.

Historic Convict Sites

An important and defining part of Tasmania is its convict history. When the British and Irish prisons were getting overcrowded in the late 18th century, many of the convicts were shipped to Australia. In July 2010, UNESCO listed 11 Australian former convict sites in its World Heritage List, 5 of which are in Tasmania.

Port Arthur Site

The historic convict site at Port Arthur - http://www.portarthur.org.au is the best known site from the convict era. Located on the south side of the Tasman Peninsula, the site was originally a timber-getting station before it was transformed into a penal colony for secondary offenders. The colony, operative between 1833 and 1877, was known for the arduous labour and strong surveillance. Prisoners were engaged in sandstone quarries and timber felling. Spread over 136 hectares in a picturesque landscape, one can see more than 30 of the convict-built structures and some ruins. The site, along with the gardens and the ruins are open from 8:30 am until sunset. There are different categories of package passes available for the entry (single day, 2 days, or late afternoon), guided tour, harbor cruise, and meals. There is no ticket for only an entry to the site.

Estates of Brickendon & Woolmers

Operative between the 1820s and the 1850s in the 2 neighbouring estates in north Tasmania, the convicts in this penal colony were assigned to private masters and were made to work on the farming fields. The male convicts were engaged as gardeners, agricultural hands, and blacksmiths, while the women were engaged as domestic maids.

The convicts were given food and clothing in exchange of their labour. The 'masters' were also responsible for the health and wellbeing of the convicts. Brickendon Estate is open between 9:30 am and 5:00 pm from Tuesday to Sunday; Woolmers Estate is open from 10:00 am to 4:30 pm every day with extended hours in summer.

Darlington Probation Station

This penal station (1825-32 & 1842-50) was located in the Maria Island National Park near the east coast. This all-male station used to categorize convicts based on their crime and subsequent behavior. The Darlington Station is the best preserved amongst the convict sites in Tasmania with 14 convict buildings and ruins spread over 361 hectares. The visiting hours are in sync with the Park's opening hours.

Coal Mines Site

Located in the Little Norfolk Bay in the north of the Tasman Peninsula, this penal colony was operational between 1833 and 1848. The prisoners were made to work in the coal mines that subsequently contributed to the development of the colony. The station was known for its severe workload and punishment. The site, spread over 214 hectares, has more than two dozen convict buildings, accommodations, and cells.

Cascades Female Factory

This all-female convict station was located in a valley at the base of Mt Wellington in Hobart. The convicts were categorized based on their crime and assigned jobs accordingly. The station had many buildings including a hospital, cook houses, workshops, church, and solitary cells. 3 of the 5 original yards along with some administrative buildings are still intact and open to the public between Monday and Friday from 9:00 am to 5:00 pm.

East Coach Beach Resorts

The east coast of Tasmania is home to not only some of the best wineries of the island but also to the best beaches of Tasmania. There are multiple award winning beach houses and eco-lodges that are lined on the pristine white beaches that open up to the beautiful turquoise waters. There are a number beaches, bays, and towns that attract thousands of tourists every year to this picturesque part of the island.

Bay of Fires

One of the most visited attractions in the east coast is the Bay of Fires. The bay got its name in 1773 from the fires lit by the native Aboriginal people that were sighted by Captain Tobias of the HMS Adventure, a part of the fleet of Captain Cook.

The bay extends from the Binalong Bay to the Edison Point and has a long stretch of white sand beaches, blue waters, and orange-coloured rocks. The northern part of the bay can be accessed through the Mount William National Park. The southern part is designated as a conservation area. The bay has many facilities for camping, fishing, swimming, and boating.

Bicheno

Located 185 km north east of Hobart, the town of Bicheno is a popular beach resort and a fishing port. The town is easily accessible by road as it is just off the Tasman Highway. The mild climate of Bicheno makes it an ideal place for not only a beach outing, but also fishing of almost every type. Cray-fishing is, in fact, the largest industry in this town. The town can be easily covered by foot and one of the best walks is from the Diamond Island to the 'blowhole'. Another stunning attraction is the abundance of penguins. Although there are regular guided tours of the penguin colonies, one may come across penguins in and around the beach areas.

St. Helens

Located on the Georges Bay, St Helens is the largest town in north east Tasmania. Located about a 2-hr drive from the Launceston Airport, St Helens is becoming an increasingly popular tourist town with its white beaches, crystal clear waters, and orange lichen-covered rocks.

Other than enjoying the beach activities and the spectacular coastal scenery, one can visit the Mt William National Park for the famous 'kangaroo drive'.

Swansea

Located about a 90-minite drive from Hobart, the town of Swansea is near the Great Oyster Bay. Other than the beaches, the town has many historic buildings including the operating century-old Morris' General Store. There are many points for swimming and surfing. Lake Leake is popular for trout fishing whereas Mayfield Beach is visited for beach and rock fishing. The scenic Meetus Falls and Lost Falls are located close to the Lake Leake. Wine lovers can also visit the vineyards in Springvale and Craige Knowe.

Other popular regions in the east coast include the Coles Bay, Maria Island, Freycinet National Park, Orford, and Pyengana.

Bruny Island

Located off the south east coast of Tasmania, Bruny Island is home to some stunning natural landscape, boutique accommodation, and unforgettable culinary delight, providing the visitor with the ultimate wilderness experience. The popular Bruny Island Cruises - http://www.brunycruises.com.au/ was named as one of the top 100 experiences by Travel and Leisure magazine.

Bruny Island is best connected from Hobart. One can fly in as the island has a small landing strip but the most popular and cheap way is to cross the D'Entrecasteaux Bay that separates the island from the Tasmanian mainland. There are ferry connections from Hobart (The Meerambeena from Kettering port) and Melbourne (The Spirit of Tasmania). Once in Bruny Island, one can use a car for travelling although many of the attractions are best seen by foot.

The island has a number of townships including Adventure Bay, Lunawanna, Barnes Bay, Simpsons Bay, Alonnah, and Dennes Point.

The island is home to the Bruny Island National Park which has a number of walking trails and bushwalks. The beach area of the island is an excellent place to spot fairy penguins, fur seals, and white wallabies. It also has many opportunities and facilities for bird watching. Bruny Island is home to Australia's southernmost vineyard as well as the southernmost licensed pub making it an ideal place for wine lovers. One can also enjoy handmade fudge, truffles, berries, and fresh oysters. The Bruny Island Cheese Company is renowned for some highly-acclaimed cheese products.

The iconic 1838 Cape Bruny Lighthouse was the oldest continuous serving lighthouse of the country and is now a part of the National Park. History lovers can visit the Bligh Museum (Adventure Bay) and the Bruny History Room (Alonnah).

Although popular as a day trip destination, Bruny Island has many facilities for accommodation at Adventure Bay and Dennes Point.

Cradle Mountain - Lake St Clair National Park

Located about 50 km inland from the north east coast of Tasmania, the Cradle Mountain - Lake St Clair National Park is part of Australia's World Heritage Wilderness Area. The Park is home to 1617m high Mt Ossa, the highest mountain of Tasmania. The Cradle Mountain area is one of the top tourist destinations on the island attracting nearly a quarter of the island visitors.

The Park was the brainchild of Gustav Weindorfer who bought some land in the area and built a chalet for his guests in 1912. By the 1930s, over 80 km of tracks were created along with guided tours on some of them. Over the years the tracks have been improved and extended. Today, there are many short and long walks in the Park that cover the major attractions like Cradle Mountain, Lake St Clair, and Dove Lake. Each walk comes with its own share of fascinating experience. The popular short walks include the Dove Lake Loop Walk (approx 1 hr), Crater Lake Circuit (2 hrs), Cradle Mountain Summit (6 to 8 hrs), and the Enchanted Walk (20 min). Helicopter flights for a scenic tour is available, details of which can be found at the visitor centre of the Park. Flight tickets cost: Adult (2 seats) at $245 each, Child - $150.

There is a shuttle bus service available inside the Park but only for those who are not using a private vehicle. Vehicle pass (for up to an 8-seat vehicle) for 24hrs cost $24.

Entry fee for the overland track is separate and costs: Adult - $200; Child (under 17 years) - $150. There is a Holiday Pass that allows entry to any Tasmanian national park for 8 weeks. The Park area has many places for accommodation ranging from campsites to private cabins.

Hastings Caves

Located in the Huon Valley – about a 90-mnite drive from Hobart – the Hastings Caves is a natural phenomenon that both fascinates and relaxes the visitors. A part of the Hastings Caves State Reserve, it encompasses a stunning dolomite cave, a rich forest reserve, and a thermal pool with relaxing warm water. Part of the reserve is the dolomite Newdegate Cave that began forming millions of years ago and has a number of richly decorated natural chambers. It stands today as Australia's most visited tourist cave and one can enjoy the experience with expert commentaries from qualified tour guides from the Wildlife Service.

The entrance to the caves was found by timber workers in 1917. The Newdegate Cave is spacious and well lit and has a total of 214 stairs in different sets. The reflection of artificial light on the white and pink crystalline dolomite makes for a magical view. One should not forget to bring cold clothes as the temperature below is maintained at a constant 9 degrees Celsius.

The thermal pool is a place for the whole family. Located amidst the forest, the pool area is equipped with picnic spot, electric barbeques, showers, and shelters. The pool water is a constant 28 degrees Celsius and is hygienically controlled. There are number of walking tracks near the thermal pool.

The Caves and Pool are open from 10:00 am to 4:00 pm with extended hours in January. Entry fee for the caves and thermal pool: Adult - $24 & $5; Child - $5 & $2.50.

The Nut at Stanley

Located on the north west coast of Tasmania, the fishing port of Stanley is today a popular tourist destination for the for its picturesque landscape and a giant volcanic plug known as The Nut. Discovered in 1798, The Nut rises 143m and has a flat top. One can take the walking route or the chairlift to the top from where there are spectacular panoramic views across the Bass Strait and the beaches. There are a number of guided tours of the area where one can spot seals, penguins, and other wildlife. Bird watching is very popular in Stanley. Tourists also visit the neighbouring beaches in Highfield with The Nut as the backdrop.

Recommendations for a Budget Traveller

Places to Stay

BIG4 Iluka

Reserve Road
Coles Bay 7215
Tel: 03 6257 0115
http://iluka-holiday-centre.tas.big4.com.au/

The BIG4 Iluka is located on the Freycinet National Park opposite Muirs Beach on the east coast.

It is built amidst the breathtaking natural landscape and provides the perfect getaway for the whole family. Berry farms and vineyards are also close to this accommodation that has free parking and free Wi-Fi. There is a variety of accommodations available ranging from campsites to private cabins. Rates start from $55 for a twin private ensuite.

Edgewater

4 Thomas Street
Devonport East 7310
Tel: 03 6427 8441
http://www.edgewater-devonport.com.au

This 3.5 star motel is just minutes away from the Devonport Ferry Terminal. It has 42 air-conditioned rooms in 2 categories – courtyard rooms for the budget conscious and waterfront and terrace rooms for those who want extra facilities and a view. All rooms are ensuite with Wi-Fi (surcharge) and tea/coffee facilities. The more expensive rooms come with ironing boards and a terrace. There is an onsite restaurant. Basic room rates start from $111 per night.

Hadley's Hotel

34 Murray Street
Hobart 7000
Tel: 03 6237 2999
 http://hadleyshotel.com.au/

This 4-star hotel is housed in an 1834 National Listed building that was built by the convicts. It is located close to the Playhouse Theatre and the Maritime Museum. It has 71 rooms with a 24hr reception and concierge service. Parking is available for a fee but Wi-Fi is free. This smoke-free hotel has a recreation room, travel desk, and in-house bar. Rooms range from standard to suite. Basic room rates start from $130 per night.

Quality Hotel

Cnr Elizabeth Street
Hobart 7000
Tel: 03 6234 6333

Located close to the Hobart city centre, it is adjacent to the Botanical Gardens. It has free parking and a travel desk. There is an onsite restaurant and a café. There is a safe deposit facility at the reception area. The hotel serves continental breakfast. Part of the renowned Choice Hotel group, room rates of this hotel starts at $110 per night.

Edinburgh Gallery B&B

211 Macquarie Street
Hobart 7000
Tel: 03 6224 9229
http://www.artaccom.com.au

This art-filled funky boutique hotel is located close to the Hobart CBD in a historic building that has been refurbished with all modern accommodation facilities. Airport drops and pickups can be arranged if requested. The hotel comes with free parking, free Wi-Fi, and a Games Room. Smoke-free rooms are available. There is a breakfast buffet. Basic room rate starts at $89, inclusive of breakfast.

Places to Eat

Cornelian Bay Boathouse

Cornelian Bay
Hobart 7000
Tel: 03 622 89289
http://www.theboathouse.com.au/

Located just minutes away from the Hobart CBD, the Boathouse restaurant is located on the bay with picture perfect views of the waterfront and the heritage listed boatshed.

It serves all the meals from breakfast to late-hour dinner. It specializes in contemporary cuisine. Lunch menu has entrees (of beef, trout, duck) priced around $20 and main non-vegetarian dishes at $30 (vegetarian at $26). Dinner menu is priced the same with some set extra menu options.

Solo Pasta & Pizza

50b King Street
Hobart 7005
Tel: 03 6234 9898
http://solopastaandpizza.com.au/

This popular and well-rated Italian eatery at the Sandy Bay is open until late hours and also has options for delivery. It has all the usual Italian delights like the pizza, calzone, pasta, and risotto. A full meal for 2 -3 persons would cost between $12 and $20. It also serves a variety of wines and some beers.

Remi de Provence

252 Macquarie Street
Hobart 7000
Tel: 03 6223 3933
http://remideprovence.com.au/

This French restaurant has the perfect setting for a quiet and relaxed meal in a chic ambience.

There are set menus that are available for lunch and dinner that is changed from time to time. The chef hails from the French province of Provence and brings authentic French styled cooking that has made this restaurant a local favourite. A meal costs about $15 per person. There is a wide variety of wines to choose from. The restaurant also serves an exquisite array of cheese.

Stillwater River

2 Bridge Road
Launceston 7250
Tel: 03 6331 4153
http://www.stillwater.com.au/

This restaurant is open for breakfast and lunch on all 7 days and for dinner from Tuesday to Saturday. Due to the popularity of this restaurant, reservations are highly recommended. This multi award winning restaurant is the perfect place for an elegant dining experience. Dishes are typically Australian with an emphasis on fresh seafood. Main dishes are priced around $30. Set menus are available for dinner along with the a la carte menu.

AAJ Indian Café & Restaurant

146/148 Charles Street
Launceston
Tel: 03 6331 9719
http://www.aajindia.com.au/

This popular Indian restaurant with a beautiful interior décor is open for dinner from 5:00 pm until 9:30 pm. Vegetarian entrees start from $7 and the non-vegetarian from$9. Indian style grilled chicken and lamb are priced about $14. There is a limited menu of condiments and desserts priced between $5 and $7. The restaurant also serves wine, beer, spirits, and soda.

Places to Shop

Island Markets

54 Gormanston Road
Hobart 7009
http://islandmarkets.com.au/

This indoor market in Moonah, Hobart, is Tasmania's largest indoor market. It is open every week from Thursday to Sunday from 9:00 am to 5:00 pm.

The Island Markets is one of the best places on the island to buy fresh produce and seafood. Between Friday and Sunday from 10:00 am until 3:00 pm, shoppers get to buy a wider variety of products including Asian groceries, plants, jewelry, handicrafts, clothing, and gift items.

Sidewalk Tribal

Castray Esplanade
Hobart 2004
http://sidewalkgallery.com.au/

Opened in the late 1980s this sidewalk gallery of African arts and crafts has become a recommended shopping attraction in Tasmania. Artworks ranging from antiques to traditional sculptures from 26 different African countries are exhibited. With real ethnic items from over 85 different African cultures at a bargain price, the Sidewalk Tribal is a must for those who are looking for something different.

Henry Jones Design Gallery

25 Hunter Street
Hobart 7000
http://www.henryjonesdesign.com.au/

Promoting Tasmanian artists and their art, the HJD Gallery has a wide variety of artworks to choose from. The eye-catching work is featured on furniture, glass, ceramic, sculpture, and jewelry. From the quirky and funky designs to the elegant and chic, there is a wide variety to choose from.

Harvest Launceston Farmers' Market

Opposite Chancellor Hotel
Launceston
http://harvestmarket.org.au/

This market is open every Saturday from 9:30 am to 12:30 pm at the Cimitiere Street car park. This farmers' market only sells food and beverages that have been grown and produced in Tasmania. It is a great place to meet and interact with locals and get a bargain on some local favourites. Visit early in the day to avoid the rush.

Design Centre Tasmania

Tamar & Brisbane Streets
Launceston
http://www.designcentre.com.au/index.php

Located next to the car park at the corner of Tamar and Brisbane streets, this gallery and sales centre has free admission. There is a spacious exhibition hall that displays the artworks along with a small sales centre. The centre promotes contemporary art mainly featured on wood. Innovative and exquisite wooden Tasmanian art pieces at an affordable price have made the centre a favourite with its guests.

MELBOURNE & TASMANIA RAVEL GUIDE

Printed in Great Britain
by Amazon